KNOWING
SELF

ZACHARY ALDEN

© 2021 Zachary Alden. All rights reserved. No part of this publication may be reproduced, distributed, or transmitted in any form or by any means, including photocopying, recording, or other electronic or mechanical methods, without the prior written permission of the publisher, except in the case of brief quotations embodied in critical reviews and certain other noncommercial uses permitted by copyright law ISBN: 978-1-09835-244-8

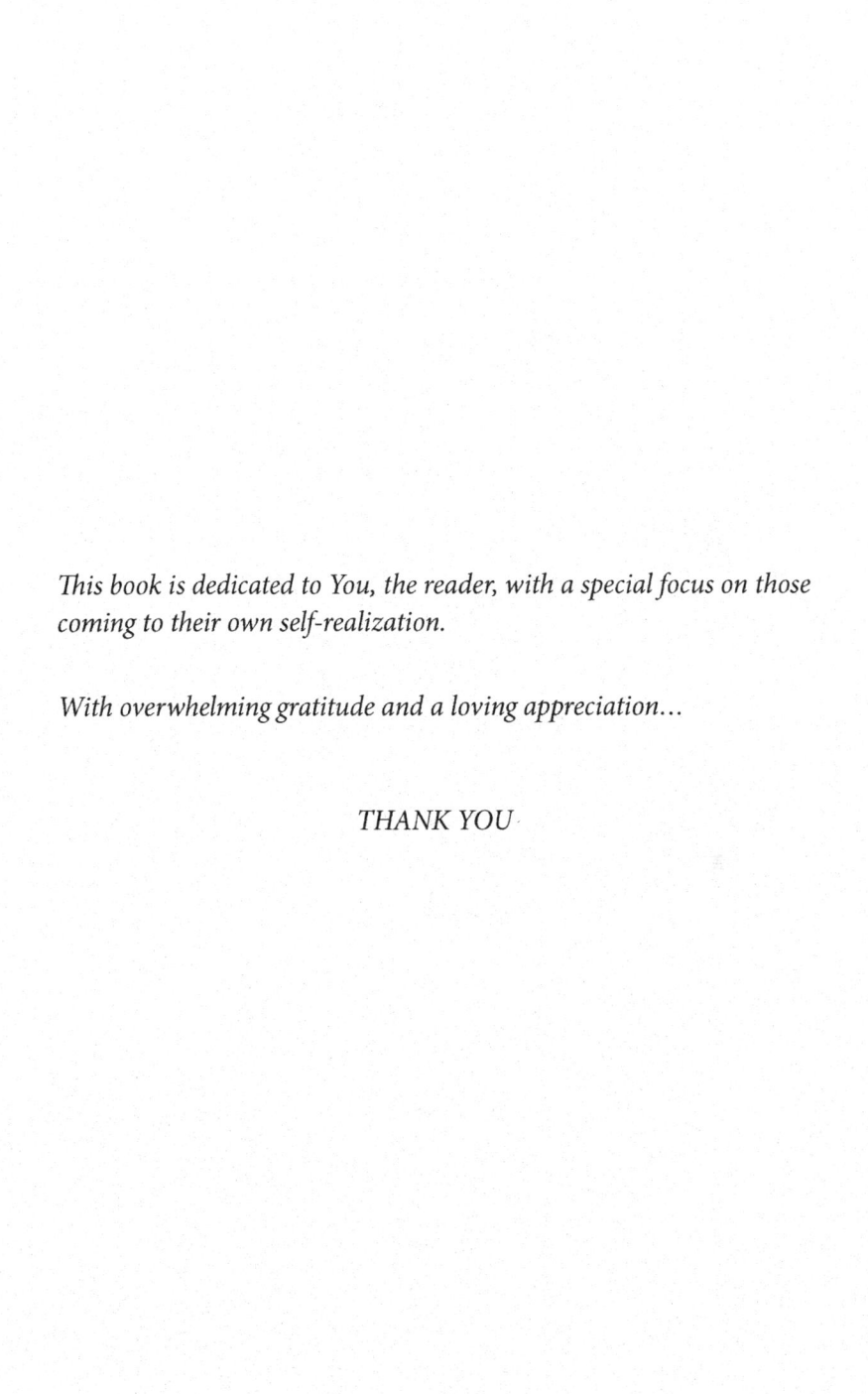

This book is dedicated to You, the reader, with a special focus on those coming to their own self-realization.

With overwhelming gratitude and a loving appreciation...

THANK YOU

Table of Contents

A Changed Perception — 2

A Flame of Opportunity — 4

Rage — 6

Suffering — 8

Searching Elsewhere — 10

Addiction — 12

Stardust — 14

A Breath of Fresh Air — 16

Light — 18

Sacred Heart — 20

Something — 22

Within — 24

The Odd Fish Out — 26

E-Motions — 28

Consciousness — 30

Mind — 32

Table of Contents

Art — 34

A Sun's Gentle Kiss — 36

Openness — 42

It — 44

The L Word — 46

The Universal Language — 48

One — 50

True — 52

Vibration — 54

An Earthy Foundation — 56

Soul's Quest — 58

All Is Nothing — 60

The Student's Teaching — 62

All the Wiser — 64

The Water-Bearer — 66

What Do You Make of It? — 68

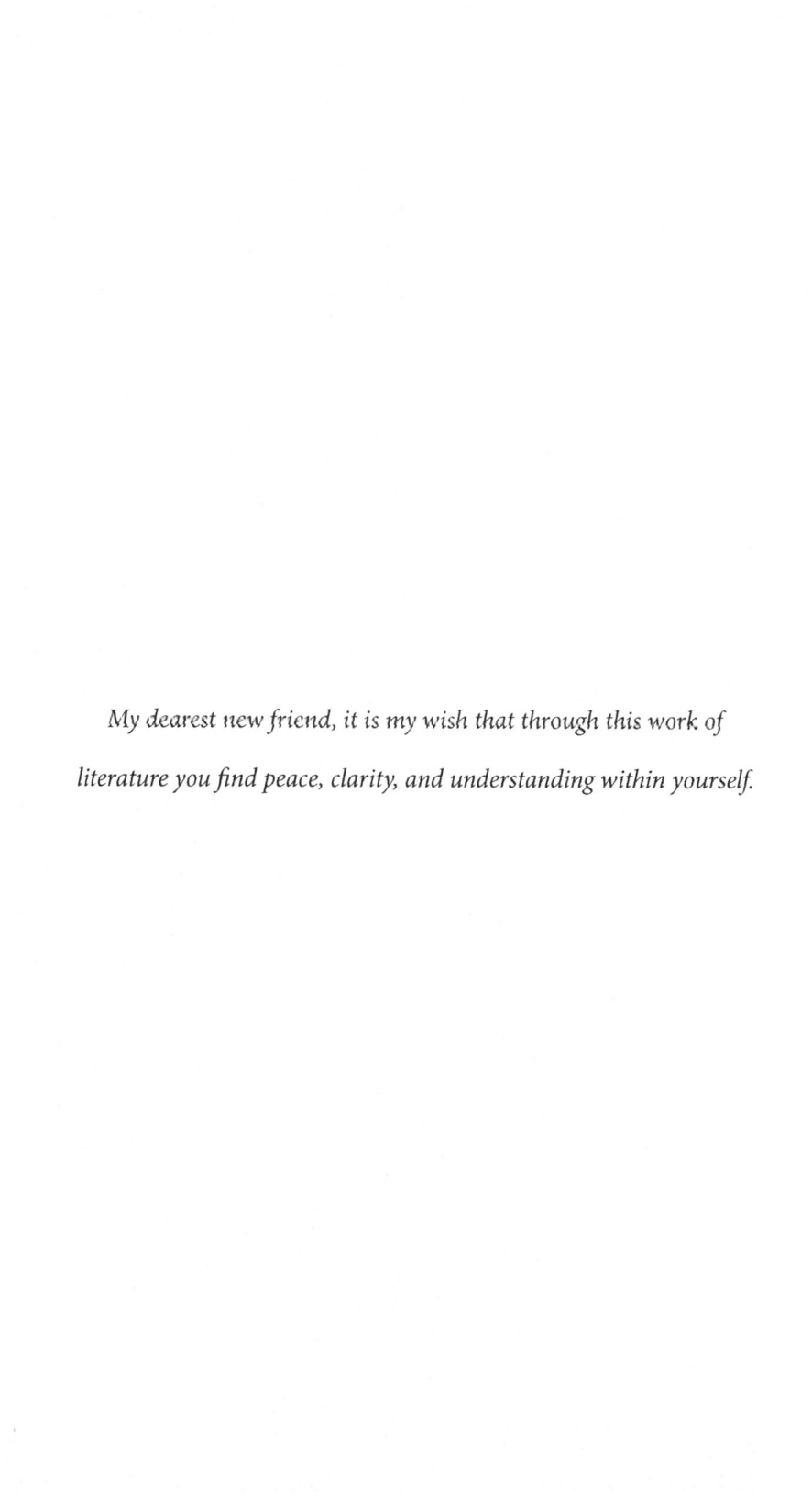

My dearest new friend, it is my wish that through this work of literature you find peace, clarity, and understanding within yourself.

The passages before you have come to fruition through my own self-reflection, personal wisdom, worldly experience, and the discovery of both One and Self. Illustrated through poetry, short stories, and metamorphic literature, this book is about the unfolding of one's vulnerability and the importance of self-love. Leaving behind the answers to one's true identity and a desire to take responsibility within One's own life, may this book be the beginning of your own self-reflection and realization.

A Changed Perception

Do you think your perception of the world will ever change?

The Human animal is created with not one but two eyes. Yet, many of us live life as if we have only one narrow eye, like that of a peephole, preventing us from seeing a possible bigger picture. Instead, we focus our energy on quite simple and limited ways of thinking, perceiving, and acting in the world. Perhaps we each have two eyes because we need to be twice as open to life's possibilities. It's time we look past what is on the other side of our self-created door of deception. Imagine if we stopped experiencing our lives through the peepholes and instead experienced this life through the people who share this world with us. They are experiencing this life just as you and I are; the only difference is their perception.

Notes of Inner Reflection

A Flame of Opportunity

When you envision a fire, what do you see? Is it a small flame from a lighter, a small pit with a warm campfire, or a large devastating forest fire? So I ask you, "Is fire a good or bad phenomenon?" The answer depends on your experience and perception of fire. For some, a fire can be a beautiful thing that provides warmth, cooks their food, even illuminates the darkness. For others, a fire might be seen as being responsible for destruction, something that only leaves scars in its aftermath. To change your perception of fire, you must change your response to it. In the scenario of a campfire, you have come to learn that a fire needs its space. With the proper response, it provides you with warmth and comfort. If you get too close, it will burn you. Your response to the fire determines your fate—whether it brings you comfort or burns you. Neither is good or bad, but simply the effect of your decision—karma. When you react without a conscious thought toward a situation, you potentially add fuel to the very thing you wish to mitigate. With a mindless reaction, you will manifest more damage; you will burn yourself out and sometimes burn the vital bridges in your life. By seeing situations as they are and adopting a more mindful approach, we can learn to grow. One can even learn to find blessings from unfortunate situations. Simply put, how you respond to situations in your life dictates the outcome, for you are only experiencing your unfortunate situation. It is entirely your response that will either make your fiery situation worse or gently calm it down. The latter will provide you with growth and warmth. Mastering this concept of the conscious response will provide more useful tool within your life. For what is a fire but one necessary tool for a tasty s'more?

Notes of Inner Reflection

Rage

Birthed from anger, grew this fire,

Through this flame, one grows tired,

Angry with self from past desires.

Wick burning quick, flamed at both ends,

Suppressed emotions, seeking amends.

Heart growing lonely, trapped in a cage,

Guarded by ego—the suffrage from rage.

Notes of Inner Reflection

Suffering

Though unique—still shared,

Details change, but life's lessons the same.

One is here, ever present,

Now as then, blind from presents,

Never sensing, that of presence.

No gifts from suffrage.

Forgiveness bears true desire.

With now as then, only suffrage.

Within Self, the will to be higher.

Notes of Inner Reflection

Searching Elsewhere

We have a habit of searching everywhere under the sun for love. We seek it both desperately and differently in each relationship and substance. Regardless, if the people reciprocate that love back to us the way we need, we love them because it benefits us and our wellbeing. We offer them guidance, give them compliments, even ask to spend time with them, all purely out of love. Though we might not get as much back from them as we give, still we press on. Hoping to crack their walls, reach their souls, shake them from the wrongdoings they hold onto. For that is what unacknowledged love is. It is the loss of self-love for oneself, created by holding onto wrongdoings and believing one is not capable or deserving of love. Can the average joe compete with an Olympian? Not unless he first turns inward and works on himself. We are all Olympic lovers, but because of life's suffering and trauma, we think we are average joes, or even less—incapable of loving ourselves or receiving it from others. So, the average joe pushes away the love so generously given to him. Only to grow lost in the world to find the love he thinks he deserves, either in someone else or a substance. So, if you are the Olympic lover, rest assured that the difficult person in your life does love you. They are just giving you love the best and only way they know how. Loving is a beautiful thing, but be mindful of who you give yourself to. The suffering souls in your life might just take your love and run, or might completely shut down and resist the love you give them. Both can be difficult to come to terms with. However, both say so much about how capable you are of loving despite getting little in return. It is better to give than receive, surely, but too much giving and nothing in return often leads to feeling like the average joe. So, be mindful of your own self-love, and despite what happens with others, know that the love you have for them is absolutely felt. One might avoid love because they do not believe they deserve it or they're scared of their own vulnerability.

So, if you think you're the average joe, the Olympian, or someone else, understand an accepting love in all that exists. All other emotions stem from love; those who lack the ability to love themselves lack the ability to love others. So, if you understand how loving you truly are, find someone you know. Someone who is looking for love in the wrong places or substances and hear their story. Understand their struggles, and love them anyway, for we all just want to be heard, we all just want to be loved.

Notes of Inner Reflection

Addiction

Entry of Twilight,

the zone of delight

veteran experience,

makes harder the flight.

Up crashing down,

Struggling to coast,

The price is found,

Still unseen in most.

Wrongly taken, still One's right,

Taken by whom, the answer to might.

Notes of Inner Reflection

Stardust

Together fallen, together flawless,

Peacefully enjoying, one's stardust,

Torn by the self, afraid of help,

Self-prevention: Quick to mention,

Those of past days, to make easy the blame.

Away, away, into the next day,

Try again, but still give blame,

Try again, still showered in pain,

For who is to blame for the self's own game?

All we are, we are all the same.

Oh, who it is, holding one's claim?

Be the same one the stardust made.

Notes of Inner Reflection

_____

_____

_____

_____

_____

_____

_____

A Breath of Fresh Air

A vital ongoing phenomenon performs as a key between inner and outer worlds: Our breath is capable of many things; through vocal vibrations, it is used to teach. This same breath of air is what gives life here on Earth. With one's inhale enters possibility, for it is life itself that is coursing through our bodies. So, when you are breathing this fresh air, are you doing so consciously, or have you forgotten this vital gift and taken it for granted? So, be more mindful with the breath that gives you life, for without the air in your breath, you wouldn't be living. So, enjoy it often, opposed to the times when you are in need of a breath of fresh air.

Notes of Inner Reflection

Light

Blind in darkness, equally by light,

To discover self but consumed of fright.

With light as Self, Self is light.

Without light, being with fright.

Without light: Being without self.

For fright is just fear.

May your unmasking be near.

Darkness, cleverly masked as our own fright.

Tread lightly towards the truth

For it's as blinding as the light.

Notes of Inner Reflection

Sacred Heart

The source of life, easily dismissed,

Nearly forgotten, without intention.

Bearing future, evermore,

Love games bear unfair scores

Over time bearing a deeper scar.

Who will fix one's broken heart?

Notes of Inner Reflection

Something

From Nothing came One.

This something, now Suns.

Forever expanding,

Forever as One.

Expanding as Nothing,

Still as something,

Something forever,

Forever as One.

Notes of Inner Reflection

Within

Deep within, oh the lie,

Patiently waiting from deep inside,

Of joy and pleasure and love, most true,

Comes shame, anger, yet growth for you.

Pain to growth—growth then glory,

Glory be that—life's purposeful journey.

So bear fruition to see one's limits,

Ended when blind, endless with vision.

Notes of Inner Reflection

The Odd Fish Out

To be one who goes against the societal norm is not an easy task. To go against the flow to create your own path will undoubtedly create friction. To be the fish who decides to start swimming upstream is challenging, as all the nearby fish are working against you. So why do it? For starters, one might act consciously in their own decision-making because they already know that all rivers lead to the ocean. So as the odd fish out, you cannot help but wonder, *What's upstream and what is the source of all this water that gives me life?*

So, you turn around and start on your own path. Doing so, you will come across far more fish, for you are now passing them as opposed to going with them. Deep down, you know:

I am not just another fish in the sea. There may be billions of people on this planet, but I am not like the rest.

So, like Dory in Nemo, you just keep swimming. Unhindered by what large rock of an obstacle lies before you, you will find a way to maneuver around it and keep swimming. It does not matter what other fish say as they swim past you for you are searching for something far greater than the average life. So, you keep swimming. Before long, talk of the odd individual who thinks differently from the rest of the fish will spread. Eventually, through your own perseverance, others will begin to approach you, not to tease you anymore but to ask, "How did you swim so far upstream?" You are no longer the odd fish out. Instead, you are something new, one that attracts the attention of others to follow, for they too are beginning to ask the question, "What is upstream?" Now, you are no longer alone.

Instead, you are surrounded by others with a like-minded curiosity. All questioning, "Is there more to life than just the ocean?"

As all fish do when they come together as one, they form a school and move together. Much like any school, each fish is now a student, together evolving as students of life and equally as teachers to those who follow. So, what does the odd fish find upstream? Well, that depends on you and how far upstream you are willing to swim.

Notes of Inner Reflection

_____

_____

_____

_____

_____

_____

_____

_____

E-Motions

The sentient experience is a vibrational fate;

The energy in motion is our emotional state.

Complex with emotions, oh what to make

Vibrations of low, leaving costly mistakes?

The being of self is one's own make

With higher vibrations comes an elevated fate.

Notes of Inner Reflection

Consciousness

A mindful doing

To prosper as truth.

Wrongly done, still yours to choose.

Freely to go, free to know,

With thoughts being conscious, the stardust grows.

Notes of Inner Reflection

Mind

For who,

The thoughts of *this* in mind?

For who,

These thoughts of that in mine?

Notes of Inner Reflection

Art

Melodies shared, deaf ears, Eye blind,

Never sensing truth in rhyme.

Time tells All,

For that we make,

Telling of this,

Soon be made.

Throughout different Art, still in pursuit,

Passionately they go, for me and You,

So Be the Human, let the Human Be.

For all Art shall soon Be that which speaks.

Notes of Inner Reflection

A Sun's Gentle Kiss

I think we all have a romance for the oceans' beaches, for they are the beginning and the ending of something far more significant than us. Just as the Sun is a sign of a new beginning, equally for day and night, both hold infinite possibilities. The beaches we love hold just as many possibilities. For without the beaches, we would not have the land.

The golden glowing sunset of Guam's Tumon Bay is without a doubt the world's most peaceful place to be every evening. The locals have a saying, "Hafa Adai" (used as hello, good day, or goodbye). The islanders don't work long hours and considering that what they're saying sounds like "half-a-day," one can only imagine they'd rather be with nature than inside working.

My love for the ocean pulled me to the beaches every evening, but it was the first evening that captured my heart. While the beaches were overly crowded, all gathering to watch the Sun fall, there was one woman who caught my eye. She was sitting on a palm tree that had fallen over; I noticed her gazing out to the horizon. The tree was long enough that I could sit by her without disturbing her. She was an older woman, perhaps old enough to be my great-grandmother. With short black hair stopping just below her ears, her curly thick hair appeared as a black helmet. Her almond-shaped eyes were a rich brown, like freshly poured pools of honey. She appeared to understand something that the rest of us forgot. Her aura: pure, calm, and inviting. I remember making eye contact as I sat down. She did not smile, but those peaceful eyes of hers smiled at me as if it was an invitation to share the fallen palm tree. In most traditional Asian cultures, the elderly are highly respected. Their well-being and hospitality are always looked out for. Knowing this, I felt a great sense of relief to see that she was welcoming of my presence.

That first night, we did not share any words, only each other's company and the commencement of the day's journey. Amazed by the peacefulness, I decided to return to the palm tree to watch the sunset the following evening. To my surprise, the elderly Korean woman was there yet again. Upon making eye contact, we both smiled and nodded to each other, acknowledging that this was now our shared place to end each other's day. Up until this point, I had no idea the significant impact sitting on a tree, watching the sunset, and admiring the vast openness of the ocean would have on my life.

The third evening rolled around, and we once again met at our palm tree, acknowledging each other's presence and enjoyed the view. She turned to me and asked how my day was. This was shocking to me given her age; I did not expect her to know English. Taken aback, I hesitated to respond. I shared with her the events of my day and expressed my disappointment that in the coming weeks, I'd have to leave. She turned to me with a soft smile and shook her head in shared dismay, paired with an understanding. Then she turned back to the ocean view. The sun was about thirty minutes from disappearing from our vision, continuing to explore past the horizon. The setting sun has a bright orange-red color with a warm and alluring captivity to it. It's as welcoming as the presence of this woman, who I still didn't know. Mesmerized by the closing sun, I, like most people my age, wanted to capture the moment for my Snapchat story. As I rushed to show the World what I was doing, I did not realize my new friend was crying.

Her tears fell softly off her cheeks and disappeared into the soft white sand at her feet. She looked at me with her still loving almond-shaped eyes and politely told me to put my phone away. Unsure of what I did to offend this gentle woman, I put my phone away and watched dozens of other people capture their fake candid photos. Sharing with the world an image of Self, only captured to be admired by others. The sun was now kissing the horizon, leaving only a few minutes of light for the day. I lovingly asked her if she was okay, and with a hopeful smile, she nodded and wished me a good night.

Over the next few days, we continued to share the palm tree, having very limited conversations and then returning our attention to the surroundings. Together, we silently admired the young loving couples, we laughed at the drunk teenagers, we listened to the music of the ocean and the laughter of the people. We hardly spoke to each other but by our shared presence alone, we both knew how the other was doing. The next evening was a Friday and knowing that I wanted to see the nighttime excitement on the beach, I arrived forty-five minutes sooner. To my surprise, there she was. Patiently sitting with an upright posture and a deep stare into the vast nothingness of the calm blue ocean. I sat down next to her and said hello. I jokingly told her I came early to spend more time with her. Regardless of the weak joke, it made her smile. Her smile shined through the thoughts that had pulled her into that deep infinite stare. This was not a soft smile like the others; it was one of love and appreciation.

Like a lotus flower in the morning sun, she bloomed openly. Without addressing her, she began to talk about herself. This was not in a flashy way but rather in a serious and open tone of significant knowledge, wisdom, and love. She shared a story of a young couple who fell deeply in love. So much in love, they ran away from their country to avoid the war, hoping they could instead make a new life with each other. The young man had a temper as hot as the sun, but beneath the rage was a soft gentle golden heart. For the man, his wife was the key to his heart, like a soft breeze or the cool refreshing waters of the morning's shore. She alone brought out the golden heart within him. Their lifelong but simple dreams were of a small family in a house on the hillside, making their ends meet by selling homegrown fresh fruit. They found their hillside home just as the local officials found them. Sadly, the officials were far more interested in the man healthy enough to be recruited for the draft than his dreams of life. Heartbroken, the young twenty-year-old couple walked the sandy beaches to collect their thoughts and enjoy the sunset together for one last time.

Sixty-two years have passed since her husband left for the war, and for those sixty-two years, that same hopeful wife has been returning to the beach to watch the sunset, waiting for his return. We sat in silence as I fully understood that this story was of her own life. In a state of pure admiration, I thanked her for coming to this beach every night. For without her, I would not have appreciated what the sunset truly is.

Before, I saw the sunset as a nice view, but now it was more than that. To everyone, it might be something different, but for myself, it's now a reminder of the love we all have for each other. Despite all the chaos of the world, each of us is always mesmerized by the beauty of a sunset. Our pains, suffering, and anger are always briefly taken away when we are truly present in the moment of the setting sun.

This profound woman, with excitement in her voice, requested to take my picture as the sun was setting. I now saw the importance of being present in the moments of awe. While most of us are quick to take a picture, post it, and forget about the full beauty of the moment, I no longer hold that ignorance. For a beautiful picture doesn't capture the sounds of laughter, the smells of the food, or the gentleness of the sand. For Mrs. Quan, the sunset over the cool water's horizon is the love she still has for her husband. For her, it's the love of a hot-tempered husband kissing his calming and reassuring wife, leaving behind a golden glow of love for all of us to admire. A love we admire as the sunset.

Notes of Inner Reflection

Openness

Surely you have heard the expression: "Closed mouths don't get fed." So, we open our mouths when we want food, or as the metaphor entails, you cannot receive what you need unless you open. The same can be said about all things once they are open. You cannot grasp or receive something unless your hand is first open. You cannot put clothes on until you open your wardrobe. In life, we use an open door to symbolize a new beginning and a closed one to symbolize an ending. The power behind openness is infinite, much like one's own imagination. But I must ask, do you think your mind is completely open? Open to all possibilities, even ones you cannot imagine? Do you fully know what is to be received with an open mind? An open door only shows you what is on the other side of the door, but until you walk past that threshold, you will not receive what's possible. Never mind what is waiting to be grasped.

Notes of Inner Reflection

It

Ever present, rarely given,

One's own doing to change with intention.

A hidden vault, cleverly hidden.

Onward death marches into life.

Onward life marches back into death.

The fabric for both, tucked in a chest.

A true treasure to find, one's very best.

What is it that we hope to find?

Lost again—in the depth of one's mind.

Notes of Inner Reflection

The L Word

The burning passion from deep within

Of Human's nature or Human sin.

The search for love, lust begins,

Left brokenhearted in beginning's end.

Continue searching,

The understanding to change,

Soon to see

What's been caged.

Notes of Inner Reflection

_____

_____

_____

_____

_____

_____

_____

The Universal Language

Currently, in the year 2020, roughly 6,500 languages are being spoken across 7.8 billion people. But that is just the human species; you must also consider the poetic sounds all the other animals make to communicate. Chirps, moos, barks, and howls—all come from vastly different animals. Yet, regardless of where you are from or what animal you are, there is a common language among all beings. For what is emotion, but a form of communication presented to the world to express the state of one's being without words? Regardless of the words said, if someone is happy or sad, you will see the difference in their eyes. Just as you can see this difference in all living things, so in this regard, we can communicate without words. If our eyes are truly the gateway to our soul and all living creatures have eyes, well, we really aren't that different, are we? More noteworthy is that we have the potential to understand all beings—even without words. So, if we are able to understand all beings, what's preventing us from changing the sorrow we see in the eyes of each other? Afterall, love is an emotion like another, and we are all seeking a loving experience through this life process. So why is it that as a society we are always seeking love for ourselves but afraid to give it to those who have the saddest eyes?

Notes of Inner Reflection

One

Seen as many,

Though forever just One,

Few will rise

From the many to come.

Waiting for the coming,

The coming of love,

The coming of this,

Is the returning to One.

Notes of Inner Reflection

True

The truth is free but wrongly caged.

Stardust's doing of emotional flames,

anger, shame, be most the blame.

But still:

It is One,

It is Self,

That carries this weight.

Knowing within, too heavy to face

The truth of being: love and grace.

Notes of Inner Reflection

Vibration

Life but a movement,

Moving to where?

Deeper we wander,

the ego does spare.

Forever moving,

Unaware of control,

Moving forever

Towards those who know.

Notes of Inner Reflection

An Earthy Foundation

The Earthly ground is an incredibly vital element of our nature. Without the Earth, we wouldn't be as we are today. Other plants and land animals wouldn't exist; it's even fair to say birds wouldn't be as they appear now. Earth's land brings an additional opportunity for life. So, in principle, the still, stable, firm, and vital ground we walk on is our first and ever-present foundation. Not just for us but for all other forms of life. Just as two people birth a child, they act as the child's primary foundation for life. So, why not be the stable, vital, and ever-present foundation for all of life, and this includes the living beings without a voice? If we create a more conscious foundation of support for all beings, what's to come of it but a more stable and loving life?

Notes of Inner Reflection

Soul's Quest

Lessons to learn, if passed with luck,

Invisible intelligence, give thanks, you must

Tests to fail with the path of prevail—

Through many, all lead the same,

This hunger to grow, despite stomachs' fat.

Self-pride and comfort, the complacent act.

Now the quest continues

Furthermore, into tomorrow,

For your time is ticking

Of which you borrowed.

Notes of Inner Reflection

All Is Nothing

To be with Nothing, to be without all,

To be as all, to be as nothing.

Together as harmony, divided let fall,

It is but Self, one's own call.

The knowing of this, is the knowing of all,

So search oneself, and let nothing now call.

Notes of Inner Reflection

The Student's Teaching

The artist understands the artist.

The musician understands the musician.

Just as the teacher understands the teacher.

The relationship between the student and the teacher is one that is far more intimate than realized. For what is a student but one willing to understand the teacher? This relationship stems from a deeper subconscious but already present understanding within the student. So, the first role of the teacher is to be the student's student. A teacher must be willing to understand their student before they can be taught. So, in this sense, we are all each other's students and each other's teachers. So, it does not matter who is sharing their wisdom; what matters is what is being said. For we are all students of life, understood as the teacher when the student is ready.

Notes of Inner Reflection

All the Wiser

Four wise men sit under the stars at night. The first turns to the other three and asks, "Gentlemen, which is wiser to seek, the question or the answer?"

The second man turns to him and replies, "You are a foolish wise man; how can one receive an answer if he doesn't ask his question?

Together, they turned to the third man for he was the wisest. He acknowledged them by saying, "A wise man answers his own question before he seeks the opinion of another."

The fourth man shared his thoughts with a smirk. "A wise man seeks other wise men. However, a wiser man knows where to seek his own answers. I did not ask a single question. Yet, each of you provided me with an answer. Merely by listening, I had answers to questions I didn't think to ask. So, you tell me, who is all the wiser from this?"

Together, the four men shared their newfound answer, and in silence, they listened for more. And because of their shared silence, they each grew all the wiser.

Notes of Inner Reflection

The Water-Bearer

The water is a busy element, effortlessly going to work and fulfilling its many duties. So, what does it mean to be like water? The most straightforward answer would be to just flow, like that of a river. Always moving forward, never looking back, and keeping a steady march towards the ocean. The ocean is not one to flow like a river. Instead, like a friendly neighbor, it waves. Those waves, continuously reaching out to the shorelines, take only a few feet of space before retreating. In this regard, being like the ocean's water only takes what you need, for you can always return for more. If the oceans frequently swept the shorelines as it does during a tsunami, we would never enjoy the ocean, so, only take what is needed and gracefully return. Then there is the rain, coming around every so often to serve a vital purpose. We tend to retreat indoors when it rains as if we have been sent to our rooms because Mother Gaia is getting to work. When it rains, the falling water washes away everything that isn't needed anymore, generously cleansing and nourishing the lands. So, be like the rain. Remember to give those in need cleansing for proper nourishment and self-growth. For if it never rained, nothing would ever grow. Lastly, there are the large bodies of water, such as ponds and lakes. Gifting life to water creatures and a playful spot for land animals. This occurs because the lakes remain calm, still, allowing all to enjoy their presence. Allowing life to unfold before itself simply by being an open and welcoming body of water. So, be water: flow, take only what is needed, cleanse and nourish, and be presently still enough to be aware of the life unfolding before you.

Notes of Inner Reflection

What Do You Make of It?

What do You label the all-loving, Divine, intelligent, energetic source that infinitely expands boundlessly across all dimensions through its own making of fractal patterns and consciousness?

What do You label as the gift within this physical realm?

What do You make of the creation that examines itself through the life process—the one that is currently observing its manifestations as the temporary but ultimate fractal pattern inept from any further division presently granted?

Whatever you make of it, it's interesting to realize that without each one, You wouldn't exist.

Notes of Inner Reflection

Life is full of lessons, only rewarding those open to its teachings.

Until next time.

Notes of Wisdom

Notes of Wisdom

Notes of Wisdom

Notes of Wisdom

Notes of Wisdom

My dearest friend…